Explore the Bible®

Let the Word dwell in you.

M000316076

BIBLE. O.T. GENESIS 12–24—STUDY

ERIC GEIGER
Vice President, Church Resources

MICHAEL KELLY
Director, Groups Ministry

AFSHIN ZIAFAT
General Editor

JEREMY MAXFIELD
Content Editor

Send questions/comments to: Content Editor, *Explore the Bible: Small-Group Study;* One LifeWay Plaza; Nashville, TN 37234-0152.

Printed in the United States of America

For ordering or inquiries visit *www.lifeway.com;* write to LifeWay Small Groups; One LifeWay Plaza; Nashville, TN 37234-0152; or call toll free 800.458.2772.

With *Explore the Bible*, groups can expect to engage Scripture in its proper context and be better prepared to live it out in their own context. These book-by-book studies will help participants—

> grow in their love for Scripture;

> gain new knowledge about what the Bible teaches;

> develop biblical disciplines;

> internalize the Word in a way that transforms their lives.

 Connect

 @ExploreTheBible

 facebook.com/ExploreTheBible

 lifeway.com/ExploreTheBible

 ministrygrid.com/web/ExploreTheBible

❯ABOUT THIS STUDY

CHANGE IS INEVITABLE. IT'S PART OF LIFE. TO GROW IS TO CHANGE.

But change isn't always easy. We often prefer the known and the comfortable to difficult challenges.

God may call us to make major changes of direction in life as we follow Him. These changes can stretch us in ways that force us out of our comfort zones and cause us to trust Him completely.

The first verses of Genesis 12 record that God called Abram to move to a new land far away. God directed him to leave the familiarity of home and go to a place he knew nothing about. He was to respond in obedience to the Lord even though it would involve life-altering changes.

Explore the Bible: Genesis—The Life of Abraham reminds us of the importance of trusting God in the big and small issues of life. This Bible study encourages us to trust God even when we don't know exactly where He's leading. We're encouraged to obey God even when that leads to difficult and uncomfortable changes. Like Abraham, each of us must choose whether we'll live the great adventure and blessing of walking with God by faith.

The *Explore the Bible* series will help you know and apply the encouraging and empowering truth of God's Word. Each session is organized in the following way.

UNDERSTAND THE CONTEXT: This page explains the original context of each passage and begins relating the primary themes to your life today.

EXPLORE THE TEXT: These pages walk you through Scripture, providing helpful commentary and encouraging thoughtful interaction with God through His Word.

OBEY THE TEXT: This page helps you apply the truths you've explored. It's not enough to know what the Bible says. God's Word has the power to change your life.

LEADER GUIDE: This final section provides optional discussion starters and suggested questions to help anyone lead a group in reviewing each section of the personal study.

For helps on how to use *Explore the Bible*, tips on how to better lead groups, or additional ideas for leading, visit:
www.ministrygrid.com/web/ExploreTheBible.

❯GROUP COMMITMENT

As you begin this study, it's important that everyone agrees to key group values. Clearly establishing the purpose of your time together will foster healthy expectations and help ease any uncertainties. The goal is to ensure that everyone has a positive experience leading to spiritual growth and true community. Initial each value as you discuss the following with your group.

❑ PRIORITY

Life is busy, but we value this time with one another and with God's Word. We choose to make being together a priority.

❑ PARTICIPATION

We're a group. Everyone is encouraged to participate. No one dominates.

❑ RESPECT

Everyone is given the right to his or her own opinions. All questions are encouraged and respected.

❑ TRUST

Each person humbly seeks truth through time in prayer and in the Bible. We trust God as the loving authority in our lives.

❑ CONFIDENTIALITY

Anything said in our meetings is never repeated outside the group without the permission of everyone involved. This commitment is vital in creating an environment of trust and openness.

❑ SUPPORT

Everyone can count on anyone in this group. Permission is given to call on one another at any time, especially in times of crisis. The group provides care for every member.

❑ ACCOUNTABILITY

We agree to let the members of our group hold us accountable to commitments we make in the loving ways we decide on. Questions are always welcome. Unsolicited advice, however, isn't permitted.

_____   _____
I agree to all the commitments.   Date

❯ GENERAL EDITOR

 **Afshin Ziafat** is the lead pastor of Providence Church in Frisco, Texas. Before assuming his current role in October 2010, Afshin spent more than a decade traveling nationally and internationally and proclaiming the gospel of Jesus Christ in churches, retreats, camps, conferences, and missions. He also helped launch Vertical Bible Study at Baylor University in Waco, Texas.

Afshin partners with Elam Ministries and regularly travels to the Middle East to train Iranian pastors. His passion is to teach the Word of God as the authority and guide for life, to preach Jesus Christ as the only Savior and Redeemer of humankind, and to proclaim the love of Christ as the greatest treasure and hope in life. He and his wife, Meredith, currently reside in Frisco, Texas, along with their daughter, Elyse.

Afshin's prayer is that by studying Genesis—specifically the life of Abraham—we too will be moved to put our faith in the God who's always faithful to His promises.

❯ CONTENTS

WHEN GOD CALLS

God called Abram to obey Him in faith.

ABOUT GENESIS

In Genesis God revealed the origins of all things except God Himself, who is eternal. Genesis 1–11 addresses big-picture events such as creation, the fall, the flood, and the formation of nations. Genesis 12–50 focuses primarily on God's creation of a covenant nation through Abraham and his descendants. This nation would be the people through whom God would eventually send the Savior, Jesus Christ. This study will explore chapters 12–22.

AUTHOR

Most conservative, evangelical Bible students agree that Moses was the human writer of Genesis, as well as the four books that follow Genesis: Exodus, Leviticus, Numbers, and Deuteronomy. While none of the five books explicitly name the author, there are references throughout the Bible to Moses' work as their writer. In particular, Jesus taught that Moses had written about Him in the law (see Luke 24:44; John 5:46).

DATE

The time of events in Genesis spans from the creation of the world (when time began) until the death of Joseph around 1804 B.C. The writer's life span can be dated around 1526 to 1406 B.C. Moses likely recorded the Book of Genesis (and the other books of the law) not long after the Israelites' exodus from Egypt around 1446 B.C. To write a faithful record of events that occurred before his time, Moses received direct revelation from God and likely also drew from carefully preserved oral histories of the patriarchs Abraham, Isaac, and Jacob.

THEME

The theme of Genesis points to the formation of a covenant people—initiated through the call of Abram/Abraham—through whom God would bless all nations. That blessing would culminate in God's sending Jesus Christ as a descendant of Abraham to provide the only way of salvation from sin. The story of God's plan to redeem fallen humanity begins in Genesis and unfolds throughout the remaining books of the Bible. Genesis provides both the context and the proper perspective for understanding where we as human beings came from, what happened to us, and where we're headed in the future.

"THE CALL OF CHRIST ON YOUR LIFE ISN'T JUST TO BELIEVE THE RIGHT THINGS ABOUT HIM BUT TO FOLLOW HIM REGARDLESS OF THE COST."
—Afshin Ziafat

› GENESIS 12:1-9

Think About It

*What's the one command
in this passage?*

*What promises
did God make?*

*What words or phrases
describe Abram's
response to the Lord?*

1 The LORD said to Abram:

> Go out from your land,
> your relatives,
> and your father's house
> to the land that I will show you.
> **2** I will make you into a great nation,
> I will bless you,
> I will make your name great,
> and you will be a blessing.
> **3** I will bless those who bless you,
> I will curse those who treat you with contempt,
> and all the peoples on earth
> will be blessed through you.

4 So Abram went, as the LORD had told him, and Lot went with him. Abram was 75 years old when he left Haran. **5** He took his wife Sarai, his nephew Lot, all the possessions they had accumulated, and the people he had acquired in Haran, and they set out for the land of Canaan. When they came to the land of Canaan, **6** Abram passed through the land to the site of Shechem, at the oak of Moreh. At that time the Canaanites were in the land. **7** Then the LORD appeared to Abram and said, "I will give this land to your offspring." So he built an altar there to the LORD who had appeared to him. **8** From there he moved on to the hill country east of Bethel and pitched his tent, with Bethel on the west and Ai on the east. He built an altar to Yahweh there, and he called on the name of Yahweh. **9** Then Abram journeyed by stages to the Negev.

UNDERSTAND THE CONTEXT

USE THE FOLLOWING PAGES TO PREPARE FOR YOUR GROUP TIME.

Moving to a new home in a faraway place can be challenging. Friends and family are left behind. The familiar is replaced with the new and different. The unknown future replaces the known past. Change can be difficult. We often prefer the known and the comfortable to difficult challenges.

Genesis 11 introduces readers to Abram, whose name God would later change to Abraham. The story of this man is very prominent through the middle of the first book of the Bible and, indeed, throughout both the Old and the New Testaments. The biblical writers and even Jesus Himself frequently refer to Abraham's story. Abraham's prominence is such that it's difficult to understand many parts of the Bible without a basic understanding of him and his story. His story is so central to the Bible's message that it aids tremendously in understanding the redemptive work of God throughout the ages.

Genesis 11 includes the genealogy leading to the birth of Abram. It traces his lineage from his ancestor Shem, the oldest son of Noah, to his father, Terah. This chapter also introduces Abram's wife, Sarai (her name later changed by God to Sarah), and his nephew, Lot.

Genesis 12 reminds us of the personal nature of God and of His desire for a personal relationship with people. He's often described in the Old Testament as "the God of Abraham, Isaac, and Jacob," reaffirming His connection with people. The theme of faith is an overarching theme found in Abraham's life and story, and the lessons of faith exemplified in his life are valuable to believers in every generation.

Hebrews 11:8-10 refers to the Genesis account of Abram's call and obedience, noting that Abram "went out, not knowing where he was going" (v. 8). The reader is reminded of the great faith required for Abram to follow the Lord into the unknown.

❯ EXPLORE THE TEXT

GOD CALLS (Genesis 12:1-3)

¹The LORD said to Abram: Go out from your land, your relatives, and your father's house to the land that I will show you.

God clearly communicated to Abram what He expected of him. There may be times when we're uncertain of what God wants us to do. Very often, however, God unmistakably tells us what to do. Through the Bible we know many specifics of what God wants us to do and to avoid. When we see God's clear Word, we're in a position to obey or disobey. God emphasized the magnitude of what He was asking of Abram. Abram was to leave the land where he lived, the family he loved, and the home he knew. The old, familiar places and many of his family and friends would be left behind. God further pointed out to Abram that he was to follow this call of obedience even though he didn't know the final destination. It was a call to faithful obedience. It was a call to trust the Lord with the future even though God hadn't revealed all the details of that future. This is a challenging call to radical obedience. The Lord asked Abram to live by faith and obey His word. There would be great change and upheaval, but the Lord was calling Abram to trust Him enough to obey Him.

What are some examples of difficult things God may call us to do today? How do these compare with the directive given to Abram?

[handwritten:] ↑ Speak up in times on disapproval to stand up to whats right.

[handwritten:] We can't see what is ahead, so it is sometimes hard to step out in faith.

[handwritten:] ↑ Pastor ↑ father / Mother ↑ Good Influence ↑ Job ↑ Obedience to God

²I will make you into a great nation, I will bless you, I will make your name great, and you will be a blessing. ³I will bless those who bless you, I will curse those who treat you with contempt, and all the peoples on earth will be blessed through you.

God spoke to Abram of the blessings that would come with obedience. God was going to make Abram into "a great nation" (v. 2). This would be fulfilled in the people of Israel who would become his descendants. Note that this was at a time when Abram and Sarai had no children. This great promise was not just for Abram alone. Abram was blessed by God in order to be a blessing to others. The interaction people had with Abram would determine their own blessings or curses. The life of obedience to the Lord results in opportunities for others to be blessed by that life or to reject those blessings. Every life lived in obedient faith to the Lord has an impact and a blessing. Not only is the individual blessed by his or her faith, but that faith also serves to bless the world as well.

This promise was fulfilled most fully in the person of Jesus. Jesus, born of the lineage of Abraham, is the means by which people of every tongue and tribe can be blessed with the greatest gift—eternal life. This promise to Abram foreshadows the coming of the Messiah who would remove the curse of sin through the cross and bless with everlasting life all who trust Him. Through Christ men and women can be set free from the bondage of sin and find the freedom that comes with salvation. The gospel message is the means by which all who are dead in sin can gain eternal life through the Lord Jesus.

KEY DOCTRINE
Evangelism and Discipleship

It's the duty and privilege of every follower of Christ and of every church of the Lord Jesus Christ to endeavor to make disciples of all nations.

In what ways has Abram's obedient faith been a blessing to the world? In what ways can our obedient faith be a blessing to others?

We can set the example for others / ~~providing the~~ Give and to help others in need, tithing Offerings

ABRAM GOES (Genesis 12:4-9)

⁴So Abram went, as the LORD had told him, and Lot went with him. Abram was 75 years old when he left Haran. ⁵He took his wife Sarai, his nephew Lot, all the possessions they had accumulated, and the people he had acquired in Haran, and they set out for the land of Canaan. When they came to the land of Canaan, …

Despite all the difficulties of following the Lord into the unknown, Abram obeyed the Lord. Simple obedience demonstrates our faith in God. Without any argument recorded, Abram followed the Lord's command. Obedience to the Lord has no age limit. Rather than arguing with the Lord about the reasons he couldn't leave his home at the age of 75, Abram simply obeyed. All the blessings that followed resulted because of this first step of faith. If Abram hadn't been willing to follow the Lord at 75, he wouldn't have seen the blessings that would come with the birth of Isaac years later. Abram didn't leave alone. What a blessing it must have been for others to join him on this great journey of faith. With only faith in God's call, Abram led this entourage to pack all they had and travel into the unknown horizon. That first step began the great adventure that would impact their lives and eternity.

In what ways might it be easier to follow the Lord as you get older? In what ways might it be more difficult?

because of expeience from the past

Weird ?

⁶Abram passed through the land to the site of Shechem, at the oak of Moreh. At that time the Canaanites were in the land. ⁷Then the LORD appeared to Abram and said, "I will give this land to your offspring." So he built an altar there to the LORD who had appeared to him.

Abram's entrance into the land of promise is marked by the recognition that "the Canaanites were in the land" (v. 6). This fact was certainly a reminder that God's plans would include some genuine adversity and possible conflict. But God reiterated His promise that this land would be given to Abram's "offspring" (v. 7). Abram's response to God's promise was worship. This was an act of faith in God's promise for the future and an act of worship to God for His presence in Abram's life. This altar, of course, was a physical structure, a tangible reminder that God had been with Abram to this point and would provide for his future. It was a visual reminder of the promises God had made for both children and land. But the altar was also a spiritual structure that stood for the faith Abram placed in the God who had promised. It represented for Abram the greatness of the Lord who was leading him into the future.

BIBLE SKILL

Notice repeated words or phrases in a Bible passage.

Biblical writers sometimes repeated key words to emphasize a theme or a message. In Genesis 12:1-3 the verb *bless* and the noun *blessing* occur several times. Another repetition in these verses is even more meaningful. Identify the two-word phrase repeated six times in these verses. (Hint: Look for a verb and its subject.)

Whom does the pronoun in this phrase denote?

What's the significance of the verb's tense?

What implication do these repeated words have for God's people today?

because it would be ~~forte~~ against the Will of God

⁸From there he moved on to the hill country east of Bethel and pitched his tent, with Bethel on the west and Ai on the east. He built an altar to Yahweh there, and he called on the name of Yahweh. ⁹Then Abram journeyed by stages to the Negev.

Abram continued the pattern of worship that would mark his life. This wasn't merely an altar where a religious ritual was performed. It was an altar where genuine worship of the Lord occurred. Though the Lord had not yet completed all His promised work in Abram's life, Abram was committed to worshiping God. Worship is an integral part of a life of faith. It's a reminder of the greatness of God, His worthiness of our praise, and the personal connection we have to Him. The long journey of Abram's obedient faith continued as his contingent of people made their way to the inhospitable desert region south of Judah. But faith in the Lord had led Abram this far, and he continued to need faith for the adventures to come.

What are some ways people today can designate or remember a meaningful time of worship?

❯ OBEY THE TEXT

God seeks people who will faithfully follow Him even if that means leaving the comfortable. God's call requires us to act on our faith even while facing risk. The blessing of God is reserved for those who demonstrate faith in Him through obedience. Worshiping God is one way to demonstrate obedience to God.

What's God asking you to do that will stretch you faith in Him? What roadblocks are keeping you from taking steps of obedience? Pray, asking God to strengthen your faith as you take the first step.

preach,

possibly start church

Think of ways your group has recently been blessed by God. How can the group use these blessings to help others? Decide on one blessing and then plan a course of action to implement it.

Evaluate your current expressions of worship. How can you worship God more wholeheartedly? How can your life also be an act of worship?

MEMORIZE

"I will bless those who bless you, I will curse those who treat you with contempt, and all the peoples on earth will be blessed through you."
Genesis 12:3

Use the space provided to make observations and record prayer requests during the group experience for this session.

MY THOUGHTS

Record insights and questions from the group experience.

_____
_____
_____
_____
_____
_____

MY RESPONSE

Note specific ways you will put into practice the truth explored this week.

_____
_____
_____
_____
_____
_____

MY PRAYERS

List specific prayer needs and answers to remember this week.

_____
_____
_____
_____
_____
_____

WAITING FOR THE PROMISE

God established His covenant relationship through Abram and his offspring.

UNDERSTAND THE CONTEXT

USE THE FOLLOWING PAGES TO PREPARE FOR YOUR GROUP TIME.

"Do you pinkie promise?" "Cross your heart and hope to die?" Perhaps you've heard children use these phrases or something similar when they want to be sure a promise will be taken seriously. Even at a young age we come to realize that not all promises are kept and that some people are more faithful in keeping their promises than others. In addition, we soon learn we aren't perfect at keeping our own promises. We might wonder whether anyone keeps their promises anymore.

We might even wonder whether God keeps His promises. Genesis 15 deals with the promises God made. God had promised Abram earlier in Genesis 12:7, "I will give this land to your offspring." In the intervening time, however, Abram and his wife, Sarai, still had no child. Perhaps Abram wondered whether God was going to keep His word. Perhaps he wondered whether he could trust God completely. God calls us to trust Him with our lives and future. He asks us to trust Him because He's trustworthy. Even when we face trials or difficulties, we can trust God to keep His word. He's a promise keeper, and He will keep His promises to us no matter how long that takes.

> "THE GOSPEL DOESN'T CALL US TO STRIVE HARDER BUT TO SURRENDER."
> —Afshin Ziafat

By Genesis 15 the text has already revealed a good deal about the faith of Abram. He left his home and followed the Lord to a land he'd never seen (see Gen. 12). He traveled to Egypt, where God protected him and his wife (see Gen. 12). His nephew, Lot, separated from him, but God continued to bless Abram (see Gen. 13). Abram rescued Lot when he was taken captive by dangerous kings (see Gen. 14). Through all of this, Abram continued a pattern of worship.

A considerable amount of time passed from God's initial promise of children and land in Genesis 12 until the events of Genesis 15. While the intervening time certainly provided evidence to Abram of God's faithfulness in other areas, the original promise of offspring to Abram had not yet been fulfilled.

❯ GENESIS 15:1-7,13-16

Think About It

Note the specific promises God made to Abram in Genesis 15.

What evidence did God give that He would keep His promises?

1 After these events, the word of the LORD came to Abram in a vision:

> Do not be afraid, Abram.
> I am your shield;
> your reward will be very great.

2 But Abram said, "Lord GOD, what can You give me, since I am childless and the heir of my house is Eliezer of Damascus?" **3** Abram continued, "Look, You have given me no offspring, so a slave born in my house will be my heir." **4** Now the word of the LORD came to him: "This one will not be your heir; instead, one who comes from your own body will be your heir." **5** He took him outside and said, "Look at the sky and count the stars, if you are able to count them." Then He said to him, "Your offspring will be that numerous." **6** Abram believed the LORD, and He credited it to him as righteousness. **7** He also said to him, "I am Yahweh who brought you from Ur of the Chaldeans to give you this land to possess."

13 Then the LORD said to Abram, "Know this for certain: Your offspring will be foreigners in a land that does not belong to them; they will be enslaved and oppressed 400 years. **14** However, I will judge the nation they serve, and afterward they will go out with many possessions. **15** But you will go to your fathers in peace and be buried at a ripe old age. **16** In the fourth generation they will return here, for the iniquity of the Amorites has not yet reached its full measure."

EXPLORE THE TEXT

ABRAM'S FRUSTRATION (Genesis 15:1-3)

¹After these events, the word of the LORD came to Abram in a vision: "Do not be afraid, Abram. I am your shield; your reward will be very great."

God told Abram, "Do not be afraid." A vision from God would be an awesome and frightening thing in itself. But it's also likely that God was telling Abram not to fear the future. In addition, God told Abram that He was his shield. A shield was an important item in warfare in the ancient world. It was used defensively to ward off the blows of the enemy's swords or arrows. It could also be used offensively to strike an enemy at close range. God wanted Abram to know that He was the shield that would protect him and enable him to win the spiritual battles of life.

God further told Abram that he was going to receive a very great reward. The Lord promised to reward Abram's faith in great ways. Rewards are spoken of in many places in the Bible. Jesus spoke of the eternal reward of service to others (see Matt. 10:42). Hebrews 11:6 tells us faith recognizes that God rewards those who seek Him. Abram certainly remembered the reward of a child that God specifically promised to him.

²But Abram said, "LORD God, what can You give me, since I am childless and the heir of my house is Eliezer of Damascus?" ³Abram continued, "Look, You have given me no offspring, so a slave born in my house will be my heir."

In verses 2-3 Abram expressed his frustration over not having a son. He told God there could be no reward for him since he didn't have a son. Instead, a servant in his house, Eliezer of Damascus, was the next in line to be his heir. Abram noted correctly but prematurely that God had given him "no offspring" (v. 3). God hadn't forgotten Abram or rescinded His promise. But His timing was certainly different from Abram's expectations.

This delay between the time God originally promised an inheritance and his present childless situation led Abram to a crisis of faith. The perceived slowness of God to keep His promise caused Abram to doubt whether God was going to keep His promise at all. When God delays in answering our prayers or in providing for our needs, we can find ourselves facing a crisis of faith. We must decide whether we'll trust the Lord even though the circumstances and timing aren't what we wish they were.

How does God's timing differ from ours? What challenges to our faith arise as a result? What benefits might there be to a delay in the fulfillment of God's promises?

GOD'S PROMISE (Genesis 15:4-5)

⁴Now the word of the LORD came to him: "This one will not be your heir; instead, one who comes from your own body will be your heir."

God responded to Abram's frustration by restating the promise He'd made long before. He promised that Abram would father a child who would be the heir of the promise. God's promise to Abram was reaffirmed in clear and certain terms. God's promises aren't restricted by our timetable. It must have seemed like an eternity to Abram as he waited for the promise to be fulfilled. But God's timing isn't always our timing.

Notice that verse 4 says "the word of the LORD" came to Abram. This wasn't merely a thought from a man or a suggestion from an angel. This was clearly the Lord's word. There's great power in recognizing the source of the words that follow. We can trust God's Word because He's the source of those words.

⁵He took him outside and said, "Look at the sky and count the stars, if you are able to count them." Then He said to him, "Your offspring will be that numerous."

God used a physical example to teach Abram a spiritual truth. He pointed out that the stars are beyond man's ability to count. Then the Lord promised that the offspring of Abram would similarly grow beyond his ability to number. God's promise must have taken on a new magnitude as Abram considered the incredible scope of God's promise. This lesson resonated with Abram, who'd undoubtedly spent many nights under the stars. He began to realize the reality of God's promise.

We can see the fulfillment of God's promise to Abram today. The Jewish people live in large numbers in Israel and many parts of the world. Those who've been adopted into God's family by faith in the Lord Jesus have become Abram's spiritual inheritance. By faith we're part of a spiritual family numbered beyond our ability to count.

List physical things that remind you of spiritual truths. Consider Bible stories and your own personal experiences.

ABRAM'S FAITH (Genesis 15:6)

⁶Abram believed the LORD, and He credited it to him as righteousness.

Verse 6 serves as a reminder that through faith we're made right with God. Though Abram had not yet experienced the promise, by faith he had appropriated it. He trusted that God was going to do everything He'd said. Faith is the means by which we can be made holy and righteous before God. Righteousness can come only by placing our faith in our perfect Savior, who perfectly forgives through His death on the cross and resurrection. By trusting Jesus, we can be made righteous and holy before God as though we'd never sinned.

BIBLE SKILL
*Use other Scripture
to help understand
a biblical truth.*

Genesis 15:6 is easily
comprehended in its
context. This verse is
quoted three times in
the New Testament to
demonstrate the validity
of more profound
biblical truth. Read
Romans 4:3; Galatians
3:6; and James 2:23.
Read several verses
before and after each
verse to understand
the context of the
quotation from
Genesis 15:6.

What do the quotations
in Romans and
Galatians say about
salvation?

What does the
quotation in James
reveal about faith?

What do these insights
disclose about Abram's
relationship with God?

How do these truths
apply to our lives today?

By faith we trust God to keep His word and to fulfill His promises. By faith we experience salvation and cleansing from sin. By faith we live lives that influence the world for the cause of Christ. God desires faith and honors faith. Through it we can be forgiven and declared holy before Him.

How would you compare Abram's response to a person's acceptance of Christ?

GOD'S PLAN (Genesis 15:7,13-16)

7He also said to him, "I am Yahweh who brought you from Ur of the Chaldeans to give you this land to possess."

God further reminded Abram of the call to follow Him from Ur of the Chaldeans to a new land. Abram had followed God by faith to this point, and God was calling for continued faith. Our past obedience and faithfulness can be a springboard for our future obedience and faithfulness. God often asks us to trust Him with the future without giving us all the specifics.

13Then the LORD said to Abram, "Know this for certain: Your offspring will be foreigners in a land that does not belong to them; they will be enslaved and oppressed 400 years."

In the midst of positive news about the future for Abram and his descendants came some disconcerting news. Abram was told that his offspring would one day be "enslaved and oppressed" in a foreign land. This revelation may have surprised Abram. After all, because all the nations of the earth were to be blessed through his offspring, Abram might have expected an easy path and future for these people.

God specified the length of time of this enslavement: four hundred years. This adversity would be for a time, yet it wouldn't last forever. Adversity is difficult for anyone. Believers can be assured of God's ultimate deliverance, either in this world or in the eternity God has planned for His children.

¹⁴However, I will judge the nation they serve, and afterward they will go out with many possessions. ¹⁵But you will go to your fathers in peace and be buried at a ripe old age. ¹⁶In the fourth generation they will return here, for the iniquity of the Amorites has not yet reached its full measure."

God told Abram the enslavement and oppression would result in judgment on the oppressors and enrichment for his offspring. It's a reminder that God doesn't abandon us even when we face difficulties.

God promised Abram a long life. This promise was certainly fulfilled; Abram lived to be 175 years old (see Gen. 25:7). God furthered the promise by stating that Abram's offspring would return to their promised home after their long captivity. Noting the "iniquity" (v. 16) of the current inhabitants, the Amorites, God said their sins would eventually result in righteous judgment. Even this promise of future judgment points us toward God's grace. He delayed this judgment for centuries as evidence of His mercy. But He also promised that judgment would eventually and assuredly come to those who rejected His love.

What do these verses reveal about God and His view of the future?
How should this understanding of God affect our trust in Him?

❯ OBEY THE TEXT

We can trust God, knowing that He has a sovereign plan even when we don't understand. Faith in God and His provision is the only path to righteousness. He reveals His plans to those who faithfully follow Him.

Reflect on things you've been waiting on from God. Identify those that are connected to God's promises in Scripture. Pray through your list, asking God either to change your desires, to reveal His plans, or to give you patience to wait.

What are some ways your Bible-study group can encourage one another to develop deeper faith? What specific steps can you take to help your group trust the Lord with your lives and future?

Consider areas where God wants you to trust Him more. Evaluate the level of faith you have in God and in His plans for your future. Identify steps you must take to strengthen your faith and to demonstrate trust in God's future for you.

MEMORIZE

"Abram believed the LORD, and He credited it to him as righteousness." Genesis 15:6

Use the space provided to make observations and record prayer requests during the group experience for this session.

MY THOUGHTS

Record insights and questions from the group experience.

_____

_____

_____

_____

_____

_____

MY RESPONSE

Note specific ways you will put into practice the truth explored this week.

_____

_____

_____

_____

_____

_____

MY PRAYERS

List specific prayer needs and answers to remember this week.

_____

_____

_____

_____

_____

_____

A NEW NAME

God is capable of fulfilling His covenant promises.

UNDERSTAND THE CONTEXT

USE THE FOLLOWING PAGES TO PREPARE FOR YOUR GROUP TIME.

Trusting God with every aspect of our lives and future can be difficult. Instead of making our own plans and asking God to bless them, He wants us to trust His plans and leading. His plans are better than ours. He wants us to seek His will rather than our own. Learning to trust God's plan is an important part of our spiritual growth.

Genesis 16 records the story of Hagar and Ishmael. Instead of trusting God, Sarai and Abram decided to make their own plan. Because Sarai doubted God's ability to give her a child, she gave her Egyptian slave, Hagar, to Abram to conceive a child. Abram agreed to this alternative plan and became the father of a son, Ishmael. This led to great turmoil. Hagar treated Sarai with contempt. Sarai responded with mistreatment of Hagar. The animosity led Hagar to run away. But the angel of the Lord appeared to Hagar and told her to go back to Sarai and Abram with the promise of many offspring. Hagar returned with a new understanding that God sees us and cares about us even when we face great difficulties and problems.

In chapter 17 God again appeared to Abram and clarified that the promised heir would be Sarai's son, not Hagar's. As a sign of Abram's calling and his covenant with God, God commanded the circumcision of Abram, his future male descendants, and his male servants. He also changed Abram's name to Abraham and Sarai's to Sarah.

Chapter 18 records Sarah's doubts that God would give her a child. She was well past childbearing years. When messengers from God came to Abraham to confirm the coming arrival of a son, Sarah laughed at the idea. When confronted with this lack of faith, she denied those doubts. God asked Abraham a key question in verse 14: "Is anything impossible for the LORD?" God asks us to trust His word and to follow His will.

"JESUS DIDN'T COME TO MAKE YOU A BETTER PERSON. HE CAME TO MAKE YOU AN ALIVE PERSON."
—Afshin Ziafat

❯ GENESIS 17:1-8,15-22

Think About It

Highlight the number of times God said, "I will."

What does the use of this statement suggest about the nature of God's plans for us?

Notice any words or phrases indicating that Abraham doubted God's trustworthiness.

What are some reasons fully trusting God can be difficult for people?

1 When Abram was 99 years old, the LORD appeared to him, saying, "I am God Almighty. Live in My presence and be blameless. **2** I will establish My covenant between Me and you, and I will multiply you greatly." **3** Then Abram fell facedown and God spoke with him: **4** "As for Me, My covenant is with you: you will become the father of many nations. **5** Your name will no longer be Abram, but your name will be Abraham, for I will make you the father of many nations. **6** I will make you extremely fruitful and will make nations and kings come from you. **7** I will keep My covenant between Me and you, and your future offspring throughout their generations, as an everlasting covenant to be your God and the God of your offspring after you. **8** And to you and your future offspring I will give the land where you are residing—all the land of Canaan—as an eternal possession, and I will be their God."

15 God said to Abraham, "As for your wife Sarai, do not call her Sarai, for Sarah will be her name. **16** I will bless her; indeed, I will give you a son by her. I will bless her, and she will produce nations; kings of peoples will come from her." **17** Abraham fell facedown. Then he laughed and said to himself, "Can a child be born to a hundred-year-old man? Can Sarah, a ninety-year-old woman, give birth?" **18** So Abraham said to God, "If only Ishmael were acceptable to You!" **19** But God said, "No. Your wife Sarah will bear you a son, and you will name him Isaac. I will confirm My covenant with him as an everlasting covenant for his future offspring. **20** As for Ishmael, I have heard you. I will certainly bless him; I will make him fruitful and will multiply him greatly. He will father **12** tribal leaders, and I will make him into a great nation. **21** But I will confirm My covenant with Isaac, whom Sarah will bear to you at this time next year." **22** When He finished talking with him, God withdrew from Abraham.

⟩ EXPLORE THE TEXT

GOD'S PROMISE RENEWED (Genesis 17:1-8)

¹When Abram was 99 years old, the LORD appeared to him, saying, "I am God Almighty. Live in My presence and be blameless. ²I will establish My covenant between Me and you, and I will multiply you greatly."

At 99 years of age, Abram received another vision from the Lord reminding him of the covenant made when Abram was 75. God identified Himself to Abram as God Almighty. The title was a reminder to Abram of God's power to keep every promise and meet every need. The Lord reminded Abram of the responsibility of obedience that comes from a personal relationship with Him. God wants us to enjoy close fellowship with Him and to obey Him.

What connection is there between our fellowship with God and our obedience to God? How does one affect the other?

³Then Abram fell facedown and God spoke with him: ⁴"As for Me, My covenant is with you: you will become the father of many nations. ⁵Your name will no longer be Abram, but your name will be Abraham, for I will make you the father of many nations. ⁶I will make you extremely fruitful and will make nations and kings come from you."

Recognizing the greatness of God, Abram bowed before Him as a sign of respect and humility. God used this occasion to reaffirm His covenant promise—a promise of land and offspring, just as He had spoken.

God also chose this moment to change Abram's name. *Abram* means *the father is exalted.* God changed his name to *Abraham,* which means *father of a multitude.* Though the promised son was not yet born, Abram's name was changed to reflect the coming reality.

God promised Abraham that he would be "the father of many nations" (v. 5). While this promise was fulfilled physically through the lineage of Isaac and Ishmael, it was also fulfilled spiritually. All believers in Christ are heirs of Abraham (see Gal. 3:7,29). He is our father by faith, and this family of faith is certainly a multitude of many.

7"I will keep My covenant between Me and you, and your future offspring throughout their generations, as an everlasting covenant to be your God and the God of your offspring after you. 8And to you and your future offspring I will give the land where you are residing—all the land of Canaan—as an eternal possession, and I will be their God."

God reiterated His promise to Abraham. The covenant would apply to the offspring of future generations. The land of Canaan that Abraham now inhabited would be the land of his future generations. God's promises make a difference in our lives. But our obedience to God also makes a difference in the lives of those who follow us. Future generations of Abraham's offspring were going to be blessed by his faithful life.

In what ways are future generations blessed by our faith? How do our choices make a difference in the lives of those who follow?

ABRAHAM OFFERED AN ALTERNATIVE
(Genesis 17:15-18)

¹⁵God said to Abraham, "As for your wife Sarai, do not call her Sarai, for Sarah will be her name. ¹⁶I will bless her; indeed, I will give you a son by her. I will bless her, and she will produce nations; kings of peoples will come from her."

God also changed Sarai's name to Sarah. He promised that Sarah was to be blessed by bearing a son. God also promised that Sarah would produce nations and kings. Sarah was a part of God's promise concerning offspring as much as Abraham was. This marriage union was a partnership in the fulfillment of God's future promises. Sarah was going to leave a legacy just as her husband would.

God blessed both husband and wife, seeing them as partners in their journey of faith and in their future blessings. God views marriage as a holy commitment and blessing. It's an institution of mutual sacrifice, respect, and love. God Himself designed it to be this way.

¹⁷Abraham fell facedown. Then he laughed and said to himself, "Can a child be born to a hundred-year-old man? Can Sarah, a ninety-year-old woman, give birth?" ¹⁸So Abraham said to God, "If only Ishmael were acceptable to You!"

Abraham laughed at the idea that Sarah would have a child. After all, he would be 100 years old and Sarah 90 years old by the time a child came. This was well past the time of expecting to equip a nursery. Instead of trusting God, Abraham came up with an alternative plan. Ishmael could become the child of promise instead of a son born to Sarah. It seemed logical. Sarah and Abraham were old; Ishmael was already born. This plan didn't require a miracle or the same level of faith. God's plan seemed so big that Abraham doubted it and tried to find an alternative.

Sometimes we want to make our own plans instead of following God's plans. We ask God to bless those plans instead of seeking what He wants. But God asks us to follow Him completely and to follow His plans fully. His plans are always better than ours.

KEY DOCTRINE
God the Father

God as Father reigns with providential care over His universe, His creatures, and the flow of the stream of human history according to the purposes of His grace.

BIBLE SKILL

Compare and contrast Scripture passages with similar phrases.

Joshua, Ezekiel, Jesus, a Samaritan leper, and John reacted to God's presence in a similar fashion to Abraham. Read Joshua 5:14; Ezekiel 1:28; Matthew 26:39; Luke 17:16; and Revelation 1:17.

What words, phrases, or concepts occur in all these verses?

How is each situation different?

What do these stories reveal about your own relationship with God?

GOD'S POWER DECLARED
(Genesis 17:19-22)

¹⁹But God said, "No. Your wife Sarah will bear you a son, and you will name him Isaac. I will confirm My covenant with him as an everlasting covenant for his future offspring."

God said no to the plans suggested by Abraham. He restated in unmistakable terms the promise of a son coming through Sarah. We must do God's will rather than follow our own will. The Lord even provided the name the son was to take—Isaac. God unmistakably planned for this child to be born to Abraham and Sarah. God doesn't want our shortcuts. He wants our faith and our obedience. We can trust Him with our future.

God told Abraham that He was going to confirm the covenant with Isaac. That is, God was keeping His covenant just as planned without any alterations or substitute plans. God's sovereignty means He's capable of doing what seems impossible to us. It also means He knows what's best for our future because He can see that future perfectly. We can trust that He holds the future securely in His powerful hands.

Why is it in our best interest that God sometimes says no to our plans? What example could you identify when God said no to someone's plans because He had a better plan for them?

²⁰"As for Ishmael, I have heard you. I will certainly bless him; I will make him fruitful and will multiply him greatly. He will father 12 tribal leaders, and I will make him into a great nation."

God didn't forget about Ishmael. Though Ishmael wasn't the promised child of the covenant, God still promised to make him the father of leaders and a great nation. Ishmael's life began when people tried to do things their way instead of God's. God's blessings on our lives aren't hindered by the difficulties of our circumstances or by the mistakes of others. The Lord can use us despite the mistakes made by our parents, relatives, or friends. He loves us despite our own past mistakes. Though we're affected by the choices of those around us, we're ultimately judged by our own choices and decisions.

²¹"But I will confirm My covenant with Isaac, whom Sarah will bear to you at this time next year." ²²When He finished talking with him, God withdrew from Abraham.

After promising to bless Ishmael, God once again promised to confirm the covenant with Isaac. Then He told Abraham that the long-awaited promised child was going to be born very soon. Verse 22 states that "God withdrew from Abraham" when this conversation ended. That is, the direct word from the Lord was spoken, and now Abraham was to act on the truth he'd been given. There comes a time when all that needs to be said has been said and we must act on the truth by faith. We can hear and learn God's Word, but we must decide to trust and act on it.

How does God assure us today? How does that assurance help us follow His plans?

❯ OBEY THE TEXT

God is capable of delivering on all His promises. Our impatience can lead us to substitute our imperfect plans for God's perfect plan. We must be careful not to limit what God can do in and through us.

Consider some ways in which you've substituted your plans for God's plans. Ask God to reveal where in your life you're doing this. Then confess your impatience and commit afresh to follow His plans.

Evaluate your level of patience while waiting for God's timing. List appropriate actions you should take while you wait. Begin to implement these actions in the next week.

List ways your Bible-study group can help one another follow God's plans and trust Him with every aspect of life. Consider practical ways to implement these ideas in the activities of your Bible-study group.

MEMORIZE

"I am God Almighty. Live in My presence and be blameless." Genesis 17:1

Use the space provided to make observations and record prayer requests during the group experience for this session.

MY THOUGHTS

Record insights and questions from the group experience.

_____
_____
_____
_____
_____
_____
_____

MY RESPONSE

Note specific ways you will put into practice the truth explored this week.

_____
_____
_____
_____
_____
_____

MY PRAYERS

List specific prayer needs and answers to remember this week.

_____
_____
_____
_____
_____
_____

WICKEDNESS AND COMPASSION

God doesn't allow disobedience and rebellion against Him to continue unrestrained. He rescues by grace alone.

UNDERSTAND THE CONTEXT

USE THE FOLLOWING PAGES TO PREPARE FOR YOUR GROUP TIME.

Children learn early in life that actions have consequences. If they disobey their parents, they get in trouble. If they run across the street without looking, there are dangers. Learning about consequences is one of the most important lessons children learn as they grow toward maturity. This is also one of the most important lessons believers can learn as they progress in Christian maturity.

Genesis 18–19 teaches us about consequences. God is just and loving, so He both rewards and disciplines. This passage talks about the love and grace of God. It also tells about the judgment that comes with disobedience and rebellion. Our choices carry consequences for good or bad. Both judgment and grace flow from the character of God, who is holy and loving.

In the interlude between God's promise to Abraham about the birth of a son in a year and the actual birth, the Bible records the story of the destruction of Sodom and Gomorrah. Three men appeared to Abraham. One was the Lord Himself in human form, and the other two were angels. God repeated the promise of a son to be born to Abraham and Sarah. Sarah overheard the conversation and laughed at the idea of giving birth at her advanced age. The Lord rebuked this doubt and reminded them that all things are possible with God.

The conversation turned to the wickedness of Sodom and Gomorrah, the nearby region where Abraham's nephew, Lot, lived with his family. Abraham asked God to spare the city of Sodom if as few as 10 righteous people could be found there. God agreed to spare the city if 10 could be found. But even such a small number wasn't to be found in Sodom.

The two angels went into the city, where they found Lot and entered his home for the night. The men of the city, however, demanded that Lot bring his guests out so that they could have sex with them. An ugly exchange followed. God's judgment on the wicked city was decreed final, and Lot and part of his family escaped the destruction of the region just in time.

"A PROPER UNDERSTANDING OF THE GOSPEL OF GRACE IS THE GREATEST FUEL FOR MISSIONS."
—Afshin Ziafat

> GENESIS 18:20-25; 19:12-16

Think About It

Look for the connection between God's judgment of sin and His expression of grace toward sinners.

What does this suggest about the nature and character of God?

Notice Lot's response to the angels' instruction.

What does his response reveal about Lot's understanding of the situation?

18:20 The LORD said, "The outcry against Sodom and Gomorrah is immense, and their sin is extremely serious. **21** I will go down to see if what they have done justifies the cry that has come up to Me. If not, I will find out." **22** The men turned from there and went toward Sodom while Abraham remained standing before the LORD. **23** Abraham stepped forward and said, "Will You really sweep away the righteous with the wicked? **24** What if there are 50 righteous people in the city? Will You really sweep it away instead of sparing the place for the sake of the 50 righteous people who are in it? **25** You could not possibly do such a thing: to kill the righteous with the wicked, treating the righteous and the wicked alike. You could not possibly do that! Won't the Judge of all the earth do what is just?"

19:12 Then the angels said to Lot, "Do you have anyone else here: a son-in-law, your sons and daughters, or anyone else in the city who belongs to you? Get them out of this place, **13** for we are about to destroy this place because the outcry against its people is so great before the LORD, that the LORD has sent us to destroy it." **14** So Lot went out and spoke to his sons-in-law, who were going to marry his daughters. "Get up," he said. "Get out of this place, for the LORD is about to destroy the city!" But his sons-in-law thought he was joking. **15** At daybreak the angels urged Lot on: "Get up! Take your wife and your two daughters who are here, or you will be swept away in the punishment of the city." **16** But he hesitated. Because of the LORD's compassion for him, the men grabbed his hand, his wife's hand, and the hands of his two daughters. Then they brought him out and left him outside the city.

◼ EXPLORE THE TEXT

MAN'S SIN (Genesis 18:20-21)

²⁰The LORD said, "The outcry against Sodom and Gomorrah is immense, and their sin is extremely serious. ²¹I will go down to see if what they have done justifies the cry that has come up to Me. If not, I will find out."

God spoke to Abraham about the wickedness of the neighboring cities of Sodom and Gomorrah. Sodom was the city where Lot, the nephew of Abraham, lived with his family. The Lord noted that the outcry against these cities was immense. The outcry could have come from victims of the sinful actions, the prayers of the righteous for deliverance from this evil, or both.

The Lord called their sinfulness "extremely serious" (v. 20). All sin is against the Lord and is therefore serious. This passage describes a pattern of rebellion. The people of the city ignored God's commands. This pattern of behavior led to the Lord's righteous judgment of them.

Our just God rightly punishes sin. Sin separates us from God and ultimately leads to pain, bondage, and death. Romans 6:23 tells us that "the wages of sin is death." That is, the consequence of sin—apart from God's grace—is eternal separation from God in hell. Without God's mercy and grace, all humankind would be under this just judgment. All stand in great need of God's grace because all have sinned against Him.

Verse 21 tells of the Lord's commitment to observe the sins of Sodom. God is a just God but never unfair. The truth always wins out in the Lord's dealings. His justice always prevails.

How is God's view of sin different from the world's view of sin? What happens when a culture ignores sin to the point that sin becomes the norm?

ABRAHAM'S INTERCESSION
(Genesis 18:22-25)

²²**The men turned from there and went toward Sodom while Abraham remained standing before the LORD. ²³Abraham stepped forward and said, "Will You really sweep away the righteous with the wicked?"**

Abraham heard the Lord speak of the seriousness of the sins of Sodom. His relationship with God led Abraham to humbly speak to God about his concerns. Our relationship with God as believers allows us to humbly intercede for others. Abraham stepped forward and asked whether the Lord would sweep away the righteous with the wicked. Abraham was calling attention to the possibility that some righteous people would suffer as a result of the destruction that was to come to the wicked. Perhaps he was concerned for his family who lived in the city.

Believers today can pray with humble boldness just as Abraham did. We can have absolute confidence that the Lord hears us when we pray. But we also pray with humility, realizing that boldness comes not on the basis of our work but through the work of Jesus Christ on our behalf. We can pray for lost and spiritually wandering family members and friends, asking the Lord to intervene in their lives.

How would you describe the way Abraham appealed to God? How did he balance humility and boldness in his approach?

²⁴"What if there are 50 righteous people in the city? Will You really sweep it away instead of sparing the place for the sake of the 50 righteous people who are in it? ²⁵You could not possibly do such a thing: to kill the righteous with the wicked, treating the righteous and the wicked alike. You could not possibly do that! Won't the Judge of all the earth do what is just?"

Abraham was specific in requesting that God spare the suffering of the righteous. He asked the Lord whether He would spare the city if 50 righteous people could be found there. In the verses that follow, Abraham gradually lowered that number to 10 righteous people in the city (see vv. 27-33). In the last sentence of verse 25, Abraham gave his rationale for the request. He recognized the Lord as the Judge of all the earth, but he also noted that the great Judge is just. While we're all affected by the sins around us, we're directly responsible for our own sins. God judges us for our actions, not for the actions of other people. Believers should recognize their personal responsibility for sin while grieving over the sinful condition of their culture and interceding for lost people. Believers can and should have a dramatic impact on the world in which they live.

What does it mean to say God is a just Judge? In what ways does the Bible demonstrate God as a just Judge?

GOD'S GRACE (Genesis 19:12-16)

¹²Then the angels said to Lot, "Do you have anyone else here: a son-in-law, your sons and daughters, or anyone else in the city who belongs to you? Get them out of this place, ¹³for we are about to destroy this place because the outcry against its people is so great before the LORD, that the LORD has sent us to destroy it."

The Lord's recognition of the wickedness in Sodom was confirmed, as was His decision to destroy the city. But He extended another act of grace. The angels asked Lot whether anyone else in Sodom was connected to Lot who could avoid the impending judgment by fleeing the city. The angels told Lot to get them out of the city. God's grace is never far removed from His judgment. The Lord was providing one last chance for those willing to take it. We too are given opportunities to avoid God's righteous judgment by repenting of our sins. The angels told Lot of the impending doom of the city. They said the outcry against the city was great and the Lord was well aware of what was transpiring there. God is always aware of the reality of the situation. He knows our sins and warns us about the danger of and damage caused by sin. These warnings are an extension of God's grace to us. A day will come, however, when His offer of grace will expire and the reality of judgment will begin.

Lot experienced an opportunity for grace when he was warned to flee the city and take those he loved. We also have an opportunity to experience God's grace as God warns us of our need for salvation. If we reject that free gift of God's love, we instead opt for God's righteous judgment against sin.

How does God's just judgment work with His offer of grace? Why is it important to understand both God's judgment and His grace?

¹⁴So Lot went out and spoke to his sons-in-law, who were going to marry his daughters. "Get up," he said. "Get out of this place, for the LORD is about to destroy the city!" But his sons-in-law thought he was joking.

Lot immediately went to his sons-in-law. Because he had compassion on these young men, he wanted them to avoid the impending disaster. A healthy understanding of God's judgment is a reason for wanting others to know the Lord as their Savior and Redeemer.

Lot's plea for his sons-in-law to leave went unheeded. They chose to stay in the culture they'd grown comfortable with rather than to experience God's better plan. Many will choose the broad path that leads to destruction instead of the narrow and more difficult path of following God's best (see Matt. 7:13).

Do you think our culture scoffs at the idea that sin carries consequences and judgment? Why or why not?

15At daybreak the angels urged Lot on: "Get up! Take your wife and your two daughters who are here, or you will be swept away in the punishment of the city." **16**But he hesitated. Because of the LORD's compassion for him, the men grabbed his hand, his wife's hand, and the hands of his two daughters. Then they brought him out and left him outside the city.

At daybreak the pleading of the angels for Lot to leave became more urgent. They encouraged him to leave quickly to escape being carried away in the judgment that was coming on the city. Verse 16 notes that Lot hesitated. We can be so accustomed to our culture that we don't notice its wickedness and fail to see the serious nature of sin. Instead of fleeing immorality as the Bible commands us, we can grow comfortable in the setting of immorality. Like Lot, we can hesitate to obey God fully.

God showed His compassion. Instead of leaving Lot behind to face certain annihilation with the rest of Sodom, the angels had mercy on Lot and his family, took them by the hand, and led them away. Through that merciful act Lot and his family were spared the destruction that came to that wicked place. The more we recognize the wickedness of sin and how undeserving of forgiveness we are, the more amazed we are at God's grace. He shows His love to us even when we hesitate and doubt. He shows His love to us even when we become accustomed to sin and lukewarm in faith. His grace is truly amazing.

❯ OBEY THE TEXT

Sin brings judgment on those who continue to rebel against God. The Lord listens to the prayers of His people, allowing them to ask about His plans. Being consistent in His character, He extends grace even in the midst of judgment.

List areas where our modern culture has significantly drifted from God's plan. Join together as a Bible-study group in praying for a return to righteousness as a nation. Pray for a revival among believers in your country, region, and church.

Ask the Lord to show you any area of sinful actions or attitudes in your personal life. Commit to full obedience to His best for your life and future.

Consider ways to show grace to others without compromising your beliefs or God's standards. Identify at least one person in your life to whom you need to show grace. List the actions you'll take to show them grace without compromising your beliefs.

MEMORIZE

"So it was, when God destroyed the cities of the plain, He remembered Abraham and brought Lot out of the middle of the upheaval when He demolished the cities where Lot had lived." Genesis 19:29

Use the space provided to make observations and record prayer requests during the group experience for this session.

MY THOUGHTS

Record insights and questions from the group experience.

_____

_____

_____

_____

_____

_____

MY RESPONSE

Note specific ways you will put into practice the truth explored this week.

_____

_____

_____

_____

_____

_____

MY PRAYERS

List specific prayer needs and answers to remember this week.

_____

_____

_____

_____

_____

_____

KEEPING HIS PROMISE

God keeps His promises and can be trusted.

⟩ UNDERSTAND THE CONTEXT

USE THE FOLLOWING PAGES TO PREPARE FOR YOUR GROUP TIME.

Genesis 21 records the fulfillment of God's promise to Abraham and Sarah. God asked them to trust Him with their future just as a child is asked to trust his father and jump into his arms. They followed Him by faith into a new land and now, years after the original promise of offspring, they saw God's promise fulfilled. Their leap of faith into the future God had for them was met by the faithfulness of the Lord in providing a son and keeping His word. God asks us to trust Him with our lives and our futures. He's strong enough to take care of us. His Word is dependable and trustworthy. He asks us to trust Him fully and completely with every part of our lives.

Twenty-five years after the original call of Abraham, God fulfilled the promise of offspring through the birth of Isaac. Several times along the way, that promise was reconfirmed. Doubts and faith intermingled in those intervening years. Doubts were expressed most strongly in the birth of Ishmael through Sarah's servant, Hagar. This circumvention of God's plan was unacceptable to God. Genesis 21:9-21 describes the departure of Hagar and Ishmael after the birth of Isaac. Though they were sent away, God promised His blessing on Ishmael but not His covenant with this son of Abraham. Faith was perhaps most strongly evidenced in the covenant relationship the Lord made with Abraham.

The core verses of this lesson are sandwiched between two stories involving a king named Abimelech, who ruled in the region of Gerar. Abraham and Sarah had moved into that region, as told in Genesis 20. The king brought Sarah into his harem after Abraham presented her as his sister. God warned Abimelech in a dream about the true nature of Abraham and Sarah's relationship. Though Abimelech hadn't touched Sarah, he confronted Abraham about the deception. We're shown again the fragility of Abraham's faith in certain instances. Finally, Genesis 21:22-34 records that Abimelech then made a covenant with Abraham after the birth of Isaac. This king recognized that God was at work in and through the life of Abraham, and he wanted a lasting agreement between their offspring. He recognized the awesome power of Abraham's God.

> "THE GOAL OF LIFE ISN'T TO EXTEND YOUR DAYS BUT TO SPEND YOUR DAYS DOING THE WILL OF GOD."
> —Afshin Ziafat

> GENESIS 21:1-8

Think About It

Observe references to time and timing in this passage.

What do these references suggest about God's trustworthiness and His concern for the details of our lives?

1 The Lord came to Sarah as He had said, and the Lord did for Sarah what He had promised. **2** Sarah became pregnant and bore a son to Abraham in his old age, at the appointed time God had told him. **3** Abraham named his son who was born to him—the one Sarah bore to him—Isaac. **4** When his son Isaac was eight days old, Abraham circumcised him, as God had commanded him. **5** Abraham was 100 years old when his son Isaac was born to him. **6** Sarah said, "God has made me laugh, and everyone who hears will laugh with me." **7** She also said, "Who would have told Abraham that Sarah would nurse children? Yet I have borne a son for him in his old age." **8** The child grew and was weaned, and Abraham held a great feast on the day Isaac was weaned.

EXPLORE THE TEXT

GOD'S PROMISE REALIZED *(Genesis 21:1-2)*

¹The LORD came to Sarah as He had said, and the LORD did for Sarah what He had promised.

There could be no doubt who was responsible for what was happening in Sarah's life. Although 25 years had passed since the promise was originally made, God kept His word. The Lord acted "as He had said" and did "what He had promised." The repetition emphasizes the certainty of God's words and actions.

This verse is a strong reminder of the trustworthy nature of the Lord. We can trust Him because He's always trustworthy. He keeps His word and His promises to His people. He doesn't mislead us or fail us. Although His timing may certainly surprise us, His faithfulness ought never to do so. He's a God who can be depended on because He's absolutely dependable.

Although Sarah and Abraham both received the promise, Sarah is singled out in this verse as one who received the fulfillment of the promise made by the Lord. God's promise to Sarah wasn't a general, generic promise but a personal one. When God makes a promise to us in His Word, we need to recognize it as a personal promise to us. His Word applies to our lives specifically and individually, not just in a general or generic sense. God desires a personal, intimate relationship with each of us.

²Sarah became pregnant and bore a son to Abraham in his old age, at the appointed time God had told him.

Just as God promised, Sarah became pregnant and gave birth to a son. This birth happened "at the appointed time," in fulfillment of the promise. That is, the birth certainly didn't fit Abraham and Sarah's expected schedule. But it was at the appointed time in God's plan. He'd planned for this event to occur at this exact moment.

Although God's timing is certainly different from human beings' timing, God is always on time. Abraham and Sarah were surprised by the timing, but God wasn't surprised in the slightest. How comforting it is for believers to recognize that God isn't surprised by the details and circumstances of our lives. He's well aware of our needs and the conditions of our lives. He fulfills His word at the right time, if not at the expected time.

You'll never face a problem that catches the Lord by surprise. You can be assured of His care and provision as you trust Him through those problems. The 25 years of waiting must have been difficult for Abraham and Sarah, but those years led to deeper faith in the Lord. Often it's to our great advantage that God allows us to wait on answers to prayer rather than answering immediately. God often blesses us through times of questions and doubts in ways we couldn't have experienced otherwise.

In what ways could Abraham and Sarah benefited because God waited 25 years to fulfill His promise to them? In what ways can God's delay in answering our prayers be a blessing?

GOD'S PROMISE REMEMBERED
(Genesis 21:3-7)

³Abraham named his son who was born to him—the one Sarah bore to him—Isaac. ⁴When his son Isaac was eight days old, Abraham circumcised him, as God had commanded him. ⁵Abraham was 100 years old when his son Isaac was born to him.

Abraham "named his son ... Isaac" (v. 3) in obedience to God's instruction (see Gen. 17:19). *Isaac* means *laughter*. Both Abraham and Sarah had laughed when God announced they'd have a child (see 17:17; 18:12). Their earlier skeptical laughter would turn into joyful laughter at Isaac's birth. The name Isaac would serve as a constant reminder to them that nothing is impossible for the Lord (see 18:14).

Abraham again followed God's word by having Isaac circumcised. This was in keeping with the covenant agreement made between the Lord and Abraham, as recorded in Genesis 17:9-14. Circumcision was the sign of the covenant established by God, and Isaac was the product of this promise.

While there are many reasons to do what the Lord wants, simple obedience is reason enough. Learning to obey God quickly and fully is a mark of a healthy believer. Abraham's prompt obedience to God in this event shows a stronger and deeper faith. The fact that Abraham was one hundred years old when Isaac was born points again to the special nature of the birth and the extended time between the original promise and its fulfillment. God keeps His promises in every circumstance.

How did Abraham's actions demonstrate faith in God? What relationship does our faith in God have to our obedience to God?

> **KEY DOCTRINE**
> *God*
>
> To God we owe the highest love, reverence, and obedience.

⁶Sarah said, "God has made me laugh, and everyone who hears will laugh with me."

Though Sarah had previously laughed at the notion of having a child at her advanced age, she now laughed for a different reason. Her laughter now came from a heart overjoyed by the birth of her son. The fulfillment of God's promise brought Sarah to a new level of trust in the Lord. She found a joy she hadn't known prior to Isaac's birth.

It's hard to keep good news to ourselves. Our joy compels us to tell others, and real joy is contagious. Sarah noted that all who heard of her good news would find reason to join her in laughter. Romans 12:15

tells us to "rejoice with those who rejoice; weep with those who weep." This was certainly the case as those who knew of Sarah's former pain now rejoiced with her at the fulfillment of God's promise.

⁷She also said, "Who would have told Abraham that Sarah would nurse children? Yet I have borne a son for him in his old age."

Sarah's connection to Abraham caused her to think of his perspective. She noted how unbelievable it would have seemed if someone had told her husband these events would happen. She particularly noted her husband's old age. While this was a tacit reminder of her own age, she spoke of it in terms of Abraham's age. She'd shared with him in this great gift of a son after the seemingly endless wait. It seemed as though they'd never have children together, and yet Isaac had been born. God had provided in an exciting and amazing way. She wasn't the only one in the family rejoicing. Isaac's birth brought joy not only to her but also to her husband. They shared this family blessing together as husband and wife.

God wants to work in us and through us regardless of our age or the circumstances of our lives. We can and should serve Him as single or married, with children or without, in every phase and situation of our lives. Living by faith and obeying the Lord's leading are for all believers in all situations.

What are inadequate excuses do people use to explain why they can't serve the Lord right now? How does Sarah's life counter those excuses?

GOD'S PROMISE REJOICED *(Genesis 21:8)*

⁸The child grew and was weaned, and Abraham held a great feast on the day Isaac was weaned.

Isaac grew and reached the age when he was weaned. This occasioned a great feast. Abraham wanted to recognize this new stage of the boy's life by hosting a large celebration reminding everyone that God had kept His promise and that Isaac was evidence of that promise kept. Not only would the celebration mark a milestone in the life of Isaac, but it also recognized the Lord's provision. All who participated in the feast would be reminded of God's promise made and kept.

We sometimes mark special occasions like birthdays and anniversaries with a celebration or a meal. Churches sometimes celebrate important milestones with events or fellowship meals. Believers can also mark special moments in life, like the salvation of a loved one or the baptism of a new Christian. These moments not only celebrate the event but also provide testimonies to others of God's faithfulness and provision. These gatherings remind us of the faithfulness of our Lord and the blessing that comes to us as we follow Him by faith.

All who gathered for this celebration for young Isaac would know the testimony of God's work in the lives of Abraham and Sarah. They'd see a God who intervenes in our lives and calls us to faith. They'd also see the results of that faith as they celebrated this special occasion in the life of the promised son.

In what ways do believers celebrate spiritual milestones in life? What are the benefits of celebrating these special moments?

› OBEY THE TEXT

God can be trusted to fulfill His promises on His timetable. We must find ways to remember God's faithfulness to us. God's provision should be celebrated as an act of worship and thanksgiving.

God keeps His promises. List actions you can take to celebrate God's faithfulness. Determine whether God has fulfilled promises for which you haven't yet taken the actions listed. Take that action or actions, recording your thoughts.

List ways people in your Bible-study group have been reminded of God's faithfulness in their lives. Note events, occasions, or special moments that have taught them that they can trust God and that God is trustworthy. Discuss how the items listed can encourage one another.

List ways God has provided for you. Share your list with a family member who may need encouragement. Take time to pray with that family member, thanking God for what He's provided for you and for him or her.

MEMORIZE

"The LORD came to Sarah as He had said, and the LORD did for Sarah what He had promised." Genesis 21:1

Use the space provided to make observations and record prayer requests during the group experience for this session.

MY THOUGHTS

Record insights and questions from the group experience.

_____
_____
_____
_____
_____
_____

MY RESPONSE

Note specific ways you will put into practice the truth explored this week.

_____
_____
_____
_____
_____
_____

MY PRAYERS

List specific prayer needs and answers to remember this week.

_____
_____
_____
_____
_____
_____

THE FAITH TEST

Abraham demonstrated faith in God's power to save.

> UNDERSTAND THE CONTEXT

USE THE FOLLOWING PAGES TO PREPARE FOR YOUR GROUP TIME.

Students have various reactions when a schoolteacher announces a test. One student may be unprepared. Perhaps he or she forgot to study or ignored the impending time of the test. This student could be nervous, worried, or doubtful. Another student might be excited about taking the test. This student is well prepared after serious study. He or she might anticipate shining academically. For good or for bad, a test can reveal what a student has or hasn't learned.

Genesis 22 records a major test of Abraham's faith—a test he couldn't have anticipated. But this test was a great opportunity for Abraham to demonstrate the lessons of faith he'd learned over the years of following the Lord. Years earlier God had called him to leave his home and travel to a land he didn't know. God had promised him offspring, only to make him wait 25 years for the birth of Isaac. This delay allowed Abraham to learn important things about faith. All those lessons now culminated in this great test. And through it Abraham would discover the depths of his own faith while God provided a foreshadowing of the greatest gift our world has ever known.

Genesis 12 began the story of Abraham's following the Lord by faith. We've seen how, at 75 years of age, Abraham was called to leave his homeland and follow the Lord into the great unknown. He was promised offspring that would be so great in number they couldn't be counted. Years went by without the fulfillment of that promise. Abraham and Sarah decided to circumvent God's plan, and this decision resulted in the birth of Ishmael. But God's plan hadn't changed. Isaac was born as the child of promise when Abraham was one hundred years old.

These events all served to teach Abraham about God's trustworthiness and to deepen his faith. Little did he know a great test of faith involving Isaac was still to come.

"WHEN THE TOUGH TIMES COME, THAT'S WHEN YOUR FAITH WILL MOST REVEAL ITSELF."
—Afshin Ziafat

❯ GENESIS 22:1-14

Think About It

Observe the way God described Isaac.

What does this suggest about the physical difficulty of God's test?

What does this suggest about the emotional difficulty of God's test?

1 After these things God tested Abraham and said to him, "Abraham!" "Here I am," he answered. **2** "Take your son," He said, "your only son Isaac, whom you love, go to the land of Moriah, and offer him there as a burnt offering on one of the mountains I will tell you about." **3** So Abraham got up early in the morning, saddled his donkey, and took with him two of his young men and his son Isaac. He split wood for a burnt offering and set out to go to the place God had told him about. **4** On the third day Abraham looked up and saw the place in the distance. **5** Then Abraham said to his young men, "Stay here with the donkey. The boy and I will go over there to worship; then we'll come back to you." **6** Abraham took the wood for the burnt offering and laid it on his son Isaac. In his hand he took the fire and the sacrificial knife, and the two of them walked on together. **7** Then Isaac spoke to his father Abraham and said, "My father." And he replied, "Here I am, my son." Isaac said, "The fire and the wood are here, but where is the lamb for the burnt offering?" **8** Abraham answered, "God Himself will provide the lamb for the burnt offering, my son." Then the two of them walked on together. **9** When they arrived at the place that God had told him about, Abraham built the altar there and arranged the wood. He bound his son Isaac and placed him on the altar on top of the wood. **10** Then Abraham reached out and took the knife to slaughter his son. **11** But the Angel of the LORD called to him from heaven and said, "Abraham, Abraham!" He replied, "Here I am." **12** Then He said, "Do not lay a hand on the boy or do anything to him. For now I know that you fear God, since you have not withheld your only son from Me." **13** Abraham looked up and saw a ram caught in the thicket by its horns. So Abraham went and took the ram and offered it as a burnt offering in place of his son. **14** And Abraham named that place The LORD Will Provide, so today it is said: "It will be provided on the LORD's mountain."

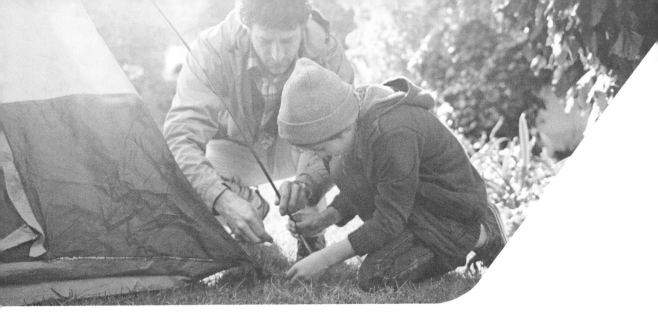

EXPLORE THE TEXT

THE TEST PRESENTED *(Genesis 22:1-2)*

¹**After these things God tested Abraham and said to him, "Abraham!" "Here I am," he answered. ²"Take your son," He said, "your only son Isaac, whom you love, go to the land of Moriah, and offer him there as a burnt offering on one of the mountains I will tell you about."**

At some point after the birth of Isaac, God came to Abraham again to test him. God called him by name, and Abraham responded with the words "Here I am" (v. 1). This is another reminder of the personal nature of the relationship God has with His followers. Abraham is personally and intimately connected with the Lord just as believers today can be.

This encounter took a twist when the Lord told Abraham to sacrifice his son. It seems unlikely that anything the Lord asked of Abraham could have been more surprising or difficult. As if to emphasize the difficulty of this assignment, Isaac was described in two ways. He was called "your only son" (v. 2). This points to the fact that Isaac was the son of the promise—the result of the covenant agreement between God and Abraham. The second description of Isaac was that he was the son "whom you love" (v. 2), indicating a strong bond of love between father and son. These two descriptions of Isaac's significance to Abraham made the command from the Lord all the more surprising. The Lord told Abraham to take his son to the land of Moriah and to offer him there as a burnt offering. God asked Abraham to sacrifice his long-awaited and dearly loved son.

This test wasn't an effort to entice Abraham to choose poorly. Rather, it was a test to prove the depth of Abraham's faith in God. The Lord used it to demonstrate how trustworthy He truly is. We can trust Him with our future plans, our families, our finances, and even our very lives.

On a scale of 1 to 10, how would you rate the difficulty of this test of Abraham's faith? List other faith tests a person could face and rate them in comparison.

THE TEST PREPARATION *(Genesis 22:3-8)*

[3]So Abraham got up early in the morning, saddled his donkey, and took with him two of his young men and his son Isaac. He split wood for a burnt offering and set out to go to the place God had told him about. [4]On the third day Abraham looked up and saw the place in the distance. [5]Then Abraham said to his young men, "Stay here with the donkey. The boy and I will go over there to worship; then we'll come back to you." [6]Abraham took the wood for the burnt offering and laid it on his son Isaac. In his hand he took the fire and the sacrificial knife, and the two of them walked on together.

Abraham began preparing for the journey early. There was no hesitancy or hint of a disobedient heart. After all, God had been trustworthy in all past dealings with Abraham, and Abraham's faith in the Lord had grown immensely. Two servants joined father and son on the journey to the mountain God had chosen. On the third day Abraham spotted the place God has designated. Abraham and Isaac left the donkey and servants behind and journeyed on in each other's company. Isaac carried the wood for the sacrifice while Abraham carried the knife and the fire.

Abraham told the two servants that he and Isaac would go worship and then come back. Note the faith demonstrated by the usage of the plural: "Then we'll come back to you" (v. 5). God had been faithful in the past. God was going to be faithful in the future, doing what seemed impossible. Though Abraham might not have fully understood how, he knew that God keeps His promises and therefore both he and his son would return—even if it meant God had to raise Isaac from the dead (see Heb. 11:19).

What did Abraham's immediate action reveal about his faith? How does the speed of obedience reveal a person's level of faith?

7Then Isaac spoke to his father Abraham and said, "My father." And he replied, "Here I am, my son." Isaac said, "The fire and the wood are here, but where is the lamb for the burnt offering?" 8Abraham answered, "God Himself will provide the lamb for the burnt offering, my son." Then the two of them walked on together.

As the father and the son walked toward the mountain, Isaac asked the obvious question: "Where is the lamb for the burnt offering?" (v. 7). Wood, fire, and a knife were there, but there was no sacrifice.

Abraham answered that God Himself would provide the lamb. Abraham couldn't have known at the time that God was going to provide another way—another lamb—for the sacrifice. Neither could he have fully understood at that moment that God would provide the ultimate sacrifice through the death of the only begotten Son of God—the Lamb who would be slain for the sins of the world (John 1:29). God provides for our needs. He sometimes provides in the everyday, usual ways. At times God provides for us through miraculous means. The death of Jesus on the cross was God's glorious provision of the all-sufficient sacrifice that takes away our sins.

THE TEST PASSED (Genesis 22:9-12)

9When they arrived at the place that God had told him about, Abraham built the altar there and arranged the wood. He bound his son Isaac and placed him on the altar on top of the wood. 10Then Abraham reached out and took the knife to slaughter his son.

God's command for Abraham to offer Isaac as a burnt offering seems out of character for God. Taken in isolation, the command in Genesis 22:2 could easily be misapplied with tragic consequences. Read Psalms 40:6-8; 51:16-17; and Hebrews 10:1-14.

What insight into God's command do these verses provide?

What principles do you see?

What do the instructions reveal about God?

What do the instructions reveal about faith?

Abraham followed God's directions in obedience. His faith wasn't just something he spoke about; his faith led to action. Abraham "bound his son" (v. 9). We can't help but wonder at the degree of faith this might have required of Isaac as well. Abraham then placed Isaac "on the altar on top of the wood" (v. 9). He took the knife in his hand and prepared to slaughter his son.

Few moments in the Bible show such tension as is seen here. Abraham was willing to obey God by faith though it meant great emotional and spiritual anguish on his part. Isaac watched the father who loved him obey the Lord in the most excruciating fashion. What a powerful moment of faith is portrayed. The connection between the faith of Abraham and the action that flowed from that faith is incredible. The Bible reveals a dynamic interaction between faith and works. The Book of Hebrews reminds us that we can't please God without faith (see Heb. 11:6), while the Book of James reminds us that faith always leads to works (see Jas. 2:14-26). What we believe is demonstrated by the actions we take.

How important is the connection between faith and works for believers today?

¹¹But the Angel of the LORD called to him from heaven and said, "Abraham, Abraham!" He replied, "Here I am." ¹²Then He said, "Do not lay a hand on the boy or do anything to him. For now I know that you fear God, since you have not withheld your only son from Me."

Just as the tension of the story reached its zenith, the angel of the Lord called out to Abraham twice. Abraham replied and listened as the angel of the Lord told him the comforting words that he wasn't to lay a hand on Isaac. Abraham had passed the test, showing that he feared God by not withholding his son. He demonstrated his strong, unwavering faith in the Lord by his actions on the mountain. He trusted God with his most precious possession and obeyed the Lord completely even in the most difficult circumstance.

What does Abraham's obedience teach us about what it means to fear God?

THE TEST PROVISION *(Genesis 22:13-14)*

¹³Abraham looked up and saw a ram caught in the thicket by its horns. So Abraham went and took the ram and offered it as a burnt offering in place of his son. ¹⁴And Abraham named that place The LORD Will Provide, so today it is said: "It will be provided on the LORD's mountain."

Not only did God spare Abraham's son, but He also provided a substitute. The ram became the burnt offering in the place of Isaac. God also provided a substitute for us. Because we're sinners, we deserve God's judgment. But Jesus is the substitutionary sacrifice for our sins. He's the Lamb who died in our place on the cross. Abraham gave a name to this spot. He called it The Lord Will Provide. The name was a reminder that God provides as we follow Him by faith. We can trust His provision for our lives and for our future. We can trust Him with all we have and all we are because His provision for our needs is assured.

How does this passage in Genesis relate to what Christ did for us on the cross? Why is it important for believers to understand the nature of Christ's sacrifice in our place?

❯ OBEY THE TEXT

God allows our faith to be tested as part of our spiritual growth. True faith is always borne out through obedient action. God provided His Son as the substitutionary sacrifice for our sins. Faith in the Son brings salvation.

List ways the members of your Bible-study group have had their faith tested. What events or periods in their lives have most tested their faith? Discuss the lessons that could be learned during those times of testing.

List the tests to your faith that you're currently experiencing. Consider what these tests are revealing about your faith in God.

Write a simple explanation of the gospel revealing that Jesus is the Lamb who died in our place on the cross. To whom do you need to communicate this truth?

MEMORIZE

"Abraham answered, 'God Himself will provide the lamb for the burnt offering, my son.' Then the two of them walked on together." Genesis 22:8

Use the space provided to make observations and record prayer requests during the group experience for this session.

MY THOUGHTS

Record insights and questions from the group experience.

_____
_____
_____
_____
_____
_____

MY RESPONSE

Note specific ways you will put into practice the truth explored this week.

_____
_____
_____
_____
_____
_____

MY PRAYERS

List specific prayer needs and answers to remember this week.

_____
_____
_____
_____
_____
_____

> ## GETTING STARTED

OPENING OPTIONS: Choose one of the following to open the group discussion.

WEEKLY QUOTATION DISCUSSION STARTER: "The call of Christ on your life isn't just to believe the right things about Him but to follow Him regardless of the cost."—Afshin Ziafat

> › What's your initial response to this week's quotation?

> › How would you explain the distinction being made between an empty belief and an active faith?

> › How is being a Christian often misrepresented as simply believing the right things about Jesus? What does this say about the value we place on following Him?

> › Today we'll begin a study in Genesis that focuses on the life of Abraham, a man who exemplifies the human experience of putting belief into action in order to follow God.

CREATIVE ACTIVITY: When the group has gathered, begin by sharing a time when you moved to a new place or started something brand-new. Share funny and heartfelt details about any awkward moments or life lessons. Then use the following to open the discussion.

> › When have you moved to a new place or situation? Briefly share what made the move or new experience memorable or significant in your life.

> › What part of that experience was the hardest? The most rewarding?

> › Today we'll begin a study in Genesis that focuses on the life of Abraham, a man who literally packed up his family without even knowing where God was moving them.

> ## UNDERSTAND THE CONTEXT

PROVIDE BACKGROUND: Briefly introduce members to Genesis and to the life of Abraham by pointing out the major themes and any information or ideas that will help them understand Genesis 12:1-9 (see pp. 7 and 9). Then, to help people personally connect today's context with the original context, use the following questions and statements.

> › Why would it have been important for God's people—the Israelites, in particular—to understand the beginning of the story about the creation of the physical world and humanity, as recorded in Genesis? Why is it still important today?

> › In Abraham (who's still called Abram at this point in the story) we see God not only continue expressing the faithfulness He'd shown since the very beginning but also make more specific promises to His people.

❯ EXPLORE THE TEXT

READ THE BIBLE: Ask a volunteer to read aloud Genesis 12:1-9.

DISCUSS: Use the following questions to discuss group members' initial reactions to the text.

> What do you like best about these verses? What do you find encouraging or challenging? What questions do you have?

> What did God call Abram to do in verse 1? What did God say He would do in verses 2-3?

> How did Abram respond in verses 4-6 to God's call and promises? How do you think the Lord's promises (count the times God said, "I will") influenced Abram's response?

> Why was God's specific promise in verse 7 significant and reassuring following the mention of the Canaanites in verse 6?

> What example does Abram provide for us with his response to the Lord in verses 7-8?

> What else do these verses teach us about God? About life?

NOTE: Provide ample time for group members to share responses and questions about the text. Don't feel pressured to prioritize the printed agenda over group members' personal experiences. If time allows, discuss responses to the questions in the personal reading.

❯ OBEY THE TEXT

RESPOND: Foster an environment of openness and action. Help individuals apply biblical truth to specific areas of personal thought, attitude, and/or behavior.

> How have you experienced God's calling? How have you responded?

> What promise of God (perhaps a favorite Scripture) is most meaningful to you and why?

> What "altars" or defining moments do you look back on to remember God's faithfulness in your life?

> What has it looked like in the past and currently for you to journey by stages in following the Lord? How can this group help you continue your journey with worship and faith?

PRAY: Close by praying for active faith and hearts of worship in each person. Ask the Spirit to open ears to hear to God's call. Pray for courage and community as you journey wherever the Lord leads you individually and as a group.

❯ GETTING STARTED

OPENING OPTIONS: Choose one of the following to open the group discussion.

WEEKLY QUOTATION DISCUSSION STARTER: "The gospel doesn't call us to strive harder but to surrender."—Afshin Ziafat

> ❯ What's your initial response to this week's quotation?

> ❯ When have you had to humbly receive help or a gift you couldn't earn or accomplish by your own effort?

> ❯ Today we'll see that Abram could do nothing to accomplish God's promises. Like Abram, we have to completely trust God, especially in times of waiting.

CREATIVE ACTIVITY: Prepare ahead of time by acquiring finger traps from a party-supply store. When the group has gathered, distribute the toys and have everyone place a finger in each end and then attempt to pull their fingers out of the trap. If you're unable to acquire finger traps, ask whether group members are familiar with the simple toy. Then use the following to open the discussion.

> ❯ What's the key to the finger-trap toy?

> ❯ When have you experienced a breakthrough when you stopped trying to accomplish something? For example, you found or remembered something as soon as you stopped looking for it or thinking about it, or a project or recognition at work finally came when you stopped trying to force success or attention.

> ❯ Today we'll see that Abram could do nothing to force God's timing. He and Sarai had to learn to rest as they waited on God.

❯ UNDERSTAND THE CONTEXT

PROVIDE BACKGROUND: Briefly introduce members to Genesis 12–15 by pointing out the major themes and any information or ideas that will help them understand Genesis 15:1-7,13-16 (see p. 17). Then, to help people personally connect today's context with the original context, use the following questions and statements.

> ❯ How might Abram and Sarai have been feeling as they continued to grow older and considerable time continued to pass without their seeing how God would make a great nation from a childless couple?

> ❯ God had proved His faithfulness and would ultimately keep His promises to them, just as He will keep His promises to us. Why is waiting on God's timing difficult?

❯ EXPLORE THE TEXT

READ THE BIBLE: Ask two volunteers to read aloud Genesis 15:1-7,13-16.

DISCUSS: Use the following questions to discuss group members' initial reactions to the text.

> What do you like best about these verses? What do you find encouraging or challenging? What questions do you have?

> In verse 1 God gave a command, a picture of His identity, and a promise. Why are the timing and nature of each significant to Abram?

> How did Abram respond in verses 2-3? What does his response reveal about a personal relationship with God?

> Verse 6 is one of the most definitive statements in all Scripture about faith. What's the relationship between belief and righteousness, as described in this verse?

> How would you explain the term *credited*? Why is it significant in the relationship between belief and righteousness? How does the word *credited* ultimately point to Jesus and faith in Him?

> In general, how would you describe the Lord's interaction with Abram in this passage? What specific details support that conclusion?

> What else do these verses teach us about God? About life?

NOTE: Provide ample time for group members to share responses and questions about the text. Don't feel pressured to prioritize the printed agenda over group members' personal experiences. If time allows, discuss responses to the questions in the personal reading.

❯ OBEY THE TEXT

RESPOND: Foster an environment of openness and action. Help individuals apply biblical truth to specific areas of personal thought, attitude, and/or behavior.

> Identify a time in your life when you could relate to Abram's confusion in trying to understand God's Word or His plan for your life.

> What fears do you need to surrender to the Lord? What questions do you currently have for God?

> How will you wait in faith for God's perfect timing in your life?

PRAY: Close by praying for God to give patience and faith to everyone in the group. Honestly express your heart. Thank Him for his faithfulness, His grace, and the righteousness He credits to us through faith in Jesus.

> ## GETTING STARTED

OPENING OPTIONS: Choose one of the following to open the group discussion.

WEEKLY QUOTATION DISCUSSION STARTER: "Jesus didn't come to make you a better person. He came to make you an alive person."—Afshin Ziafat

> What's your initial response to this week's quotation?

> In what ways do Christianity and gospel presentations often focus on changing behavior and promising benefits rather than on a new identity as a person who was saved from sin and eternal death to abundant and eternal life?

> Personally, how have you been more focused on morality and religious behavior than on the freedom and joy of your identity in Christ as a child of God, your Father?

> Today we'll see God give Abram and Sarai new names—Abraham and Sarah—to reflect their new identities according to His covenant.

CREATIVE ACTIVITY: Prepare ahead of time by finding an example of something you've unsuccessfully tried to fix or by searching the Internet for images of "funny do it yourself" or "fixed-it fails." (Always exercise caution, apply content filters, and use discernment with what you click on or view online). When the group has gathered, begin by sharing the ridiculous messes that were made from failed attempts at do-it-yourself work. Then use the following to open the discussion.

> When have you made a complete mess of something when you tried to fix it yourself? How was the problem finally resolved?

> When have you tried to take matters into your own hands in confusion or impatience instead of trusting God's timing?

> Today we'll see Abram and Sarai make a mess by taking matters into their own hands.

> ## UNDERSTAND THE CONTEXT

PROVIDE BACKGROUND: Briefly introduce members to Genesis 16–18 by pointing out the major themes and any information or ideas that will help them understand Genesis 17:1-8,15-22 (see p. 27). Then, to help people personally connect today's context with the original context, use the following questions and statements.

> How did Abram's and Sarai's actions reveal a lack of faith, even though they're remembered throughout history as godly people of faith? How can you relate to their efforts to fix things?

> How did their actions with Hagar lead to a dire problem instead of the desired solution?

> Let's see how God responded to what they did and the subsequent promises He made to them.

❯ EXPLORE THE TEXT

READ THE BIBLE: Ask two volunteers to read aloud Genesis 17:1-8,15-22.

DISCUSS: Use the following questions to discuss group members' initial reactions to the text.

> ❯ What do you like best about these verses? What do you find encouraging or challenging? What questions do you have?

> ❯ What's the significance of God's giving Abram and Sarai new names—Abraham and Sarah? How do their new, God-given identities relate to the Lord's promises and purposes?

> ❯ What specifically did God initiate and promise to do in these verses?

> ❯ According to the language in these verses, does the covenant God established depend on any conditions or behaviors? What does this unconditional covenant say about God's character and promises? What hope would it have given Abraham?

> ❯ In verses 18-20 how would you describe Abraham's request? How would you describe God's response and action toward Ishmael?

> ❯ What else does this text teach us about God? About life?

NOTE: Provide ample time for group members to share responses and questions about the text. Don't feel pressured to prioritize the printed agenda over group members' personal experiences. If time allows, discuss responses to the questions in the personal reading.

❯ OBEY THE TEXT

RESPOND: Foster an environment of openness and action. Help individuals apply biblical truth to specific areas of personal thought, attitude, and/or behavior.

> ❯ When did God give you a new identity, transforming your life by His grace? Briefly share your testimony of God's mercy.

> ❯ What difficult choices are you facing this week or in the near future?

> ❯ How will the promises of God determine your actions?

PRAY: Close by thanking God for making us all new creations through faith in Christ Jesus. Thank Him for His mercy and forgiveness of our mistakes and times when we lack faith. Ask for wisdom to live out our new identities in the name of Christ.

LEADER GUIDE—SESSION 4

❯ GETTING STARTED

OPENING OPTIONS: Choose one of the following to open the group discussion.

WEEKLY QUOTATION DISCUSSION STARTER: "A proper understanding of the gospel of grace is the greatest fuel for missions."—Afshin Ziafat

> ❯ What's your initial response to this week's quotation?

> ❯ In what ways is grace a more sustainable motivator than duty, guilt, or pity when dealing with people, especially people who are different from you in some way?

> ❯ Today we'll see how Abraham appealed to God's grace, interceding for a godless community that faced judgment.

CREATIVE ACTIVITY: When the group has gathered, begin by sharing a story about a time when things didn't work out as planned. Share humorous and frustrating details. Explain that sometimes the things we pray for don't work out exactly as we hope. Then use the following to open the discussion.

> ❯ When have you interceded in prayer, desperately pleading with God on someone else's behalf? Did God immediately answer your prayer the way you wanted? If not, how have you learned to trust God?

> ❯ Today we'll see Abraham's passionate plea, interceding on behalf of others—both family members he loved and sinful people he didn't know personally.

❯ UNDERSTAND THE CONTEXT

PROVIDE BACKGROUND: Briefly introduce members to Genesis 18–19 by pointing out the major themes and any information or ideas that will help them understand Genesis 18:20-25; 19:12-16 (see p. 37). Then, to help people personally connect today's context with the original context, use the following questions and statements.

> ❯ When have you laughed, like Sarah, at the thought of God's doing something that seemed impossible?

> ❯ How do we see the Lord's faithfulness in visiting Abraham and Sarah with the angels?

> ❯ Notice the stark contrast when the angels' conversation suddenly transitioned from the Lord's faithfulness and blessing according to His covenant to His righteous judgment and punishment for sin. How were both of these consistent with God's character?

❯ EXPLORE THE TEXT

READ THE BIBLE: Ask two volunteers to read aloud Genesis 18:20-25 and 19:12-16.

DISCUSS: Use the following questions to discuss group members' initial reactions to the text.

> ❯ What do you like best about these verses? What do you find encouraging or challenging? What questions do you have?

> ❯ How do we see both grace and justice in the Lord's visit with Abraham? With Lot and his family in Sodom and Gomorrah?

> ❯ What do these passages teach us about sin?

> ❯ How does Genesis 19:14 epitomize most people's attitude toward judgment? Toward the warnings and commands and God's Word? Toward the gospel offering salvation?

> ❯ In Genesis 18:23-25 what does Abraham's boldness reveal about prayer?

> ❯ In the verses following Abraham's initial plea, he continued to negotiate with the Lord (see 18:26-33), progressively lowering the number to only 10 righteous men. What does this conversation reveal about God's patience and His desire to show mercy?

> ❯ What else do these verses teach us about God? About life?

NOTE: Provide ample time for group members to share responses and questions about the text. Don't feel pressured to prioritize the printed agenda over group members' personal experiences. If time allows, discuss responses to the questions in the personal reading.

❯ OBEY THE TEXT

RESPOND: Foster an environment of openness and action. Help individuals apply biblical truth to specific areas of personal thought, attitude, and/or behavior.

> ❯ How seriously do you take your own sin? The sin of others?

> ❯ What would change if the Lord visited you right now, promising to spare you, your family, and others in your community?

> ❯ For whom can you pray this week to experience God's salvation, being spared His judgment? What steps will you take to share the gospel of grace with them?

PRAY: Close with a time of confession of sin, silent or aloud. Thank God for saving us by grace and finding us righteous through faith in Jesus, our Lord. Intercede for specific people to repent of their sin and to be saved from eternal judgment.

LEADER GUIDE—SESSION 5

❯ GETTING STARTED

OPENING OPTIONS: Choose one of the following to open the group discussion.

WEEKLY QUOTATION DISCUSSION STARTER: "The goal of life isn't to extend your days but to spend your days doing the will of God."—Afshin Ziafat

> ❯ What's your initial response to this week's quotation?

> ❯ In what ways are you preoccupied with your earthly future—next stages in life like continuing education, career, family, investments, and retirement?

> ❯ In what ways are you intentionally seeking to understand and do the will of God?

> ❯ Today we'll see how after years of learning to trust God's will and live by faith, Abraham and Sarah experienced the blessing the Lord promised.

CREATIVE ACTIVITY: Prepare ahead of time by creating a picture that represents the greatest experience in your life. When the group has gathered, display the picture and briefly tell a story about the happiest day of your life. Include a few details about your joy and any surprise, hardship, or waiting that made the moment even more rewarding. Then use the following to open the discussion.

> ❯ What was your happiest moment and why?

> ❯ Today we'll see the joy of Abraham and Sarah as they experienced the joy of giving birth to the child God had promised 25 years earlier.

❯ UNDERSTAND THE CONTEXT

PROVIDE BACKGROUND: Briefly introduce members to Genesis 20–21 by pointing out the major themes and any information or ideas that will help them understand Genesis 21:1-8 (see p. 47). Then, to help people personally connect today's context with the original context, use the following questions and statements.

> ❯ What's the longest you've ever waited for something? What emotions, doubts, or mistakes did you wrestle with as you waited?

> ❯ Abraham and Sarah waited 25 years between the time they first followed God's call to leave their home and the birth of Isaac. They didn't always making wise or godly decisions along the way as they wrestled with how God would protect and provide for them as He promised.

❯ EXPLORE THE TEXT

READ THE BIBLE: Ask a volunteer to read aloud Genesis 21:1-8.

DISCUSS: Use the following questions to discuss group members' initial reactions to the text.

> ❯ What do you like best about these verses? What do you find encouraging or challenging? What questions do you have?

> ❯ In verses 1-4 how many times does a form of the phrase "as God said/told/promised" appear? What does this repeated statement intentionally emphasize?

> ❯ Why was the birth of this child so miraculous?

> ❯ How would you describe Sarah's response (see vv. 6-7)? How would you describe Abraham's response (see vv. 4,8)?

> ❯ Why are laughter, celebration, and feasting important? Why are they significant components of our relationship with God like faith, prayer, patience, and suffering?

> ❯ What else do these verses teach us about God? About life?

NOTE: Provide ample time for group members to share responses and questions about the text. Don't feel pressured to prioritize the printed agenda over group members' personal experiences. If time allows, discuss responses to the questions in the personal reading.

❯ OBEY THE TEXT

RESPOND: Foster an environment of openness and action. Help individuals apply biblical truth to specific areas of personal thought, attitude, and/or behavior.

> ❯ In what ways can God's perfect timing result in a delay in fulfilling His promise? How have you experienced the joy of God's answering a longtime prayer?

> ❯ How have you been able to tell that story, sharing the laughter, like Sarah, with all who hear of God's faithfulness and blessing?

> ❯ Like Abraham, how will you personally celebrate this week the blessings God has given to you?

PRAY: Close by encouraging everyone to voice a simple word or sentence prayer of thanks, praising God for specific blessings in their lives. Praise God for His miraculous work in you and through you. Ask the Lord to continue using your lives to spread the great news of Jesus, the Promised One and the ultimate fulfillment of the promise made to Abraham and the nation descended from Isaac.

> ## GETTING STARTED

OPENING OPTIONS: Choose one of the following to open the group discussion.

WEEKLY QUOTATION DISCUSSION STARTER: "When the tough times come, that's when your faith will most reveal itself."—Afshin Ziafat

> › What's your initial response to this week's quotation?

> › How have you experienced incredible hardship that revealed your source of hope and security? How did it ultimately point you to total dependence on Christ and God's Word?

> › Today we'll see the ultimate test of faith.

CREATIVE ACTIVITY: Prepare ahead of time by gathering physical objects or images of things that are seemingly unchangeable. When the group has gathered, begin by passing around the objects or displaying the images. Then use the following to open the discussion.

> › What other things in life seem unchangeable?

> › When have you faced a crisis because something changed that you never expected to change?

> › Everything in this world changes over time. Natural features like canyons, mountains, or bodies of water slowly rise or erode. Man-made objects eventually break or wear down. Even jobs, homes, and relationships aren't guaranteed. Today we'll see that only God's character and promises are unchanging. He alone is worthy of complete devotion and ultimate hope.

> ## UNDERSTAND THE CONTEXT

PROVIDE BACKGROUND: Briefly introduce members to Genesis 22 by pointing out the major themes and any information or ideas that will help them understand Genesis 22:1-14 (see p. 57). Then, to help people personally connect today's context with the original context, use the following questions and statements.

> › How would you summarize what we've learned over the previous five sessions about the lives of Abraham and Sarah?

> › How has completing this study the past several weeks been an example of God's timing and faithfulness?

> › Today we'll conclude our study with the climax of Abraham's story—his intense crisis of faith; his total surrender to God's will; and God's perfect timing, provision, and faithfulness.

❯ EXPLORE THE TEXT

READ THE BIBLE: Ask a volunteer to read aloud Genesis 22:1-14.

DISCUSS: Use the following questions to discuss group members' initial reactions to the text.

> What do you like best about these verses? What do you find encouraging or challenging? What questions do you have?

> How would you describe the intensity of the struggle Abraham (and Issac) must have experienced? What's revealed by the faithful obedience of Abraham in these verses? What example did he set for believers today?

> What was the significance of sacrifice in the time of Abraham?

> Ultimately, God didn't require the sacrifice of Abaham's son—the promised child of God's covenant and blessing to all nations. Though God never required or allowed a human sacrifice, how does this story ultimately point to Jesus, God's only Son and the sacrificial Lamb of God?

> What else do these verses teach us about God? About life?

NOTE: Provide ample time for group members to share responses and questions about the text. Don't feel pressured to prioritize the printed agenda over group members' personal experiences. If time allows, discuss responses to the questions in the personal reading.

❯ OBEY THE TEXT

RESPOND: Foster an environment of openness and action. Help individuals apply biblical truth to specific areas of personal thought, attitude, and/or behavior.

> How have you experienced God's miraculous and perfectly timed provision?

> How are you currently trusting God to provide?

> Are you experiencing a crisis of faith, and time seems to be running out for God's provision? Are you confused about what you should do to obey His will?

> How can we pray for and encourage you to put everything in God's hands, even in the toughest times?

PRAY: Close by praying for any specific prayer needs or struggles mentioned. Thank God for specific ways He's provided for tangible needs in your lives. Praise the Lord for providing not only the ram in place of Isaac, Abraham's son, but ultimately the ultimate and final sacrifice in our place—the Lamb of God, Jesus, God's Son.

❯TIPS FOR LEADING A GROUP

PRAYERFULLY PREPARE

Prepare for each session by—

> ❯ **reviewing the weekly material and group questions ahead of time;**
> ❯ **praying for each person in the group.**

Ask the Holy Spirit to work through you and the group discussion to help people take steps toward Jesus each week as directed by God's Word.

MINIMIZE DISTRACTIONS

Create a comfortable environment. If group members are uncomfortable, they'll be distracted and therefore not engaged in the group experience. Plan ahead by taking into consideration—

> ❯ **seating;**
> ❯ **temperature;**
> ❯ **lighting;**
> ❯ **food or drink;**
> ❯ **surrounding noise;**
> ❯ **general cleanliness (put pets away if meeting in a home).**

At best, thoughtfulness and hospitality show guests and group members they're welcome and valued in whatever environment you choose to gather. At worst, people may never notice your effort, but they're also not distracted. Do everything in your ability to help people focus on what's most important: connecting with God, with the Bible, and with others.

INCLUDE OTHERS

Your goal is to foster a community in which people are welcome just as they are but encouraged to grow spiritually. Always be aware of opportunities to—

> ❯ **invite** new people to join your group;
> ❯ **include** any people who visit the group.

An inexpensive way to make first-time guests feel welcome or to invite people to get involved is to give them their own copies of this Bible-study book.

ENCOURAGE DISCUSSION

A good small group has the following characteristics.

> **Everyone participates.** Encourage everyone to ask questions, share responses, or read aloud.

> **No one dominates—not even the leader.** Be sure what you say takes up less than half of your time together as a group. Politely redirect discussion if anyone dominates.

> **Nobody is rushed through questions.** Don't feel that a moment of silence is a bad thing. People often need time to think about their responses to questions they've just heard or to gain courage to share what God is stirring in their hearts.

> **Input is affirmed and followed up.** Make sure you point out something true or helpful in a response. Don't just move on. Build personal connections with follow-up questions, asking how other people have experienced similar things or how a truth has shaped their understanding of God and the Scripture you're studying. People are less likely to speak up if they fear that you don't actually want to hear their answers or that you're looking for only a certain answer.

> **God and His Word are central.** Opinions and experiences can be helpful, but God has given us the truth. Trust Scripture to be the authority and God's Spirit to work in people's lives. You can't change anyone, but God can. Continually point people to the Word and to active steps of faith.

KEEP CONNECTING

Think of ways to connect with members during the week. Participation during the session is always improved when members spend time connecting with one another away from the session. The more people are comfortable with and involved in one another's lives, the more they'll look forward to being together. When people move beyond being friendly and in the same group to truly being friends who form a community, they come to each session eager to engage instead of merely attending.

Encourage group members with thoughts, commitments, or questions from the session by connecting through—

> emails;
> texts;
> social media.

When possible, build deeper friendships by planning or spontaneously inviting group members to join you outside your regularly scheduled group time for—

> meals;
> fun activities;
> projects around your home, church, or community.

❯GROUP CONTACT INFORMATION

Name _____ Number _____

Email/social media _____

Name _____ Number _____

Email/social media _____

Name _____ Number _____

Email/social media _____

Name _____ Number _____

Email/social media _____

Name _____ Number _____

Email/social media _____

Name _____ Number _____

Email/social media _____

Name _____ Number _____

Email/social media _____

Name _____ Number _____

Email/social media _____

Name _____ Number _____

Email/social media _____

Name _____ Number _____

Email/social media _____

Name _____ Number _____

Email/social media _____